Notes on
The Next Attention

Notes on
The Next Attention

Chandolin, 1993–2000

Fran Shaw, Ph.D.

Indications Press
New York

Copyright © 2010 Fran Shaw, Ph.D.

All rights reserved. No part of this book may be reproduced, translated, stored in or introduced into a retrieval system, or transmitted, in any form, or by any means (electronic, mechanical, photocopying, recording, or otherwise, including scanning, uploading, or distributing via the Internet) without the prior written permission of the copyright owner. For inquiries, please send an email to info@thenextattention.com.

To order books, go to www.thenextattention.com.

The words "Faith of consciousness is freedom" (p. 1) are from G. I. Gurdjieff's *Beelzebub's Tales to His Grandson*, New York: Viking Arkana, 1992 edition, p. 330.

Author's Note: All other quotations (including everything set in Optima) are my best recollection of what Michel de Salzmann said during the many years I had the opportunity to listen to him. I was not privy to any written or recorded material nor am I aware that any such material exists.

Book and jacket design by Yuko Uchikawa
Jacket art by R. David Shaw
Photographic portrait of Michel de Salzmann (p. ii)
  by Jan Clanton Collins and Sue Kagan
Other photographs by Jim and Aubrey Paull

Published with the permission of Alexandre de Salzmann

Library of Congress Cataloging-in-Publication Data

Shaw, Fran Weber, 1947-
 Notes on The Next Attention : Chandolin, 1993-2000 / by Fran Shaw.
   p. cm.
 ISBN 978-0-9639100-8-0
1. Spirituality. 2. Salzmann, Michel de. 3. Gurdjieff, Georges Ivanovitch, 1872-1949. I. Title.
 BL624.S495 2010
 197--dc22
                           2009007970

For Michel and all of his companions

CONTENTS

Preface	1
First Look	7
The Next Attention: Working with Michel	9

Week One

Monday

Everything We Need Is Here in Us	41
To Let the Experience Open	45
Sensation as a Ground so Attention Can Stay	49
Free Attention—Not Taken by Anything	53

Tuesday

Correspond to This Sacred Attention	57
Whatever Comes, I Am Free	61
Concentrating Requires Determination	65

Wednesday

One Can Have a Look Upon Oneself	69
Let Go of Ideas	73
Consciousness Is Contagious	77

Thursday

We Are Reminders for Each Other	81
To Be with This Other Person	85
I Begin To Feel My Responsibility	89

Friday

Absolutely Objective, Like the Sun	93
Recognize These Two Worlds	97
With a Very Active Attention	101

Saturday

Suddenly, This Contact with a Higher Energy	105
What Comes First Is Attention	109
This Intelligence That Is Not Mine	113
What Is Still Is the Attention	117

Sunday

What Is the Change in Us?	121
An Inner Sun Begins To Appear	125
Letting Impressions Be Received	129
Sensitivity Everywhere	133

Week Two

Monday

Acceptance Is "Energetical"	139
Join This Attention	143
The Moment of Relation with Something Finer	147
This Touch of Energy	151

Tuesday

Not To Analyze Your Functions	155
Respect When the Energy Is There	159
Come Toward the Source	163
A Taste of Truthfulness	167

Wednesday

It Is Possible Precisely When I Cannot	171
What You Give Depends on What You Receive	175
Contact with an Intelligence	179

Thursday

Authentic Self Can Emerge	183
You Are Called To Attend	187
What the Body Is For	191

Friday

An Energy That Permeates with Full Authority	195
Ascent and Descent, the Same Energy	199
Seeing Allows This Other Energy To Appear	203
It Is the Inner Life That Breathes	207

Saturday

Every Hour, To Align	211
Come Back to This Quiet in You	215
Awaken This Sense of Presence	219
The Attention Is Always There	223

Sunday

Freedom in a Moment	227
The Only Way Out Is Up	231
Love Is Not a Speech about Love	235
Everything Feeds This Sense of Presence	239

Week Three

Monday

To Serve This Intelligence	245
Be "In the Middle"	249
Join This World of Presence	253
The Now Contains Everything	257

Tuesday

Resistance Is Just Being Engaged Elsewhere	261
Am I That?	265
There Are Two Kinds of Self-Love	269

Wednesday

When There Is a Relation with the Source	273
Life Helps You Work	277
Pay with Your Attention	281
Speak from the Love of It	285

Thursday

Come Under Another Influence	289
This Mutually Freer State	293
The Interloper and the One Who Is Aligned	297

Friday

Let a Feeling Arise for Consciousness	301
Recognize This Energy	305
A Demand on Oneself To Appear	309
Is It Possible Now?	313

Saturday

Let This Flow of Life Penetrate	317
In the Silence, Wish Can Appear	321
Sensitive to the Attention Behind	325
The Real Force in Me	329

Sunday

Nothing Belongs to Me	333
When Something Real Is Received, Wish Arises	337
Opening to the Unknown Frees Me	341
Be Fully a Channel for That	345

You Can Receive the Whole World:
A Talk with Young People   349

Afterword: A Great Gift   357

In full quietness,
    Breathing in.
In full quietness,
    Breathing out.
Aware of the world,
    Breathing in.
Aware of the world,
    Breathing out.

PREFACE

An alpine village in the summer sunlight. The long dirt road carved out of the mountain. A rocky path down to a cluster of small buildings. On a Sunday afternoon, ninety strangers, young and old, from half a dozen countries, arrive at a chalet in Chandolin, Switzerland, to live together for one week in very close quarters: women in dorms, men in a large tent, with some assigned to sleep in the rafters above the dining hall. Carved in French on one rafter: "Faith of consciousness is freedom."

For many years, here and around the world, Dr. Michel de Salzmann would meet with groups interested in the Work, the teaching brought by G. I. Gurdjieff for awakening oneself in the midst of everyday life. I worked with Michel (as he preferred to be called) during the last decade of his life. In Switzerland and New York, I began writing down the words I heard him say that helped me most, both for myself and for friends unable to attend. Some of what is here was said to me in private, some to small groups of us asking questions, some at mealtimes or in discussions with everyone, and some in sittings (guided meditation). In short, this book is a distillation of my best recollections of what Michel said over several years as he worked with us Americans.

When Michel spoke, he galvanized our listening with concentrated alertness. Immediately afterward, I would sit by myself and write what I could without paraphrasing. So these assembled passages have gaps and sometimes jump from one thing to another. No one took notes or made recordings during meetings, so there is no way to be sure these are the exact words of Michel. Yet people who knew Michel say it is his voice they hear, and I hope that is true. It is important to add that what is printed here was intended for a particular audience, at a particular time, and limited by the level of the instrument receiving the impressions. I am grateful to Michel's son Alexandre de Salzmann for granting permission to publish these notes.

Even though English was not Michel's first language, and his sentences were not always complete, his meaning was clear. The word *work*, here, refers to active attention, "free from all my concerns" and subtle enough, perhaps, to join for a moment the Intelligence of the cosmos. Seeing objectively, being present, "related to an energy"—all these are prominent themes.

∽

Each "Week" draws on material from more than one year (1993-2000). The arrangement by "Days" gives the feeling of a week's progression. For want of a better term, I call these groupings of sentences "talks," but they are not an attempt to reproduce lectures: none were given. All of Michel's comments were spontaneous and informal, prompted by the state of things at the moment. I have tried to bring his exact words, which were always inventive, and to capture the cadence of his speaking. Fixing his English to elucidate an idea was not an option because what is conveyed here is not conceptual: it's "energetical."

The intention is to take the reader to Chandolin to hear Michel and experience what some of us heard and try to live: this bringing together of awakened consciousness and our everyday selves. We would come with our baggage, according to type, and our difficulties would be washed away in moments of attention, or as Michel puts it,

> All these forces in me that usually have their way in my ordinary state because there is no higher force there—now all are drawn up in the current. Ego, features, are still there, but now they serve. And when they serve the higher force, all is changed....

> With attending to presence, allowing higher forces to enter, staying collected, returning, we can live in a new way.

A week with Michel gave us a taste of a new way to live.

    Readers interested purely in Michel's words, and the vibration they carry, can skip the introduction and go right to the heart of the book: the "talks."

    Readers engaged in yoga, meditation, or mindfulness practice will find resonances in what Michel brings, a teaching he (and Gurdjieff) call *haida yoga*, that is, rapid yoga. "As human beings," Michel tells us, "we have the capacity for another dimension to appear simultaneously with all this that thinks, feels, reacts." Perhaps there is already contact with "the inexhaustible dimension" of attention:

> Even a little bit of conscious energy is like gold from which something can start…. When there is attention, the body is light. Not brutal in action, speech. Sensitivity appears naturally.

In fact, "Everything we need is here in us. Everything for fuller being."

How is it, then, that a more conscious state does not last? I try to *be*—yet surely *being* cannot mean having "a nice experience and then you are passive again."

What is the process of waking up?

Michel draws a distinction between something *I do* with my attention and something *received*. He speaks of a quality of Attention that is "a sacred energy coming into me":

> With a very active attention, I can receive this energy…. When this energy is there and I am sure of it, aware of it moment by moment, I begin to *be*.

Indeed, "the only discovery is this energy":

> We are in a process to come under another influence. There is "my" attention, secondary attention, that runs up the mountain, sees obstacles, does this or that…. If it is "my" attention, it is not this other Attention, which *transforms*.

"This other Attention"—which transforms—is the subject of this book.

FIRST LOOK

On a high alpine slope: the twin-peaked rooftops of a brown chalet, with a small cement patio behind. Just below, down the hill, the little chalet. In front of it, a terrace bounded by a low stone wall where the land drops off steeply to a meadow dotted with flowers.

Alongside the large chalet, a stone walkway adjoins the dining hall. A bell hangs at the entrance.

Lush pines cover the slopes. In the distance, at the extreme left, jagged snow peaks; as the haze clears, one in particular that looks from this angle like a face in profile: the Matterhorn.

No one in sight. A place at rest, in silence.

THE NEXT ATTENTION: WORKING WITH MICHEL

Lugging one's bags down the path to the chalet on a hot July afternoon. It has been a long journey to arrive, by invitation, here at "camp": years of meeting in groups, sitting, practicing inner exercises, and taking mindfulness tasks as reminders during the day to wake up. One comes with the usual plumage of ego and beliefs, wanting to live consciously but at the same time protecting one's image. It is for the supportive atmosphere of many trying to awaken, with the help of a guide, that one crosses an ocean.

For those new to Chandolin, the week progresses like an ascending musical scale rising from the initial *do* on arrival to a higher *do* at week's end—an octave of transformation. Some people go through intervals of difficulty at the same time. By midweek, each day brings more moments when one is aware of—no word for it—the life force flowing through one's body and all around; one learns to pay attention to that. At week's end, everything one thinks about oneself, everything one knows, is nothing—usual mind, not what transforms.

Hallelujah!

It is as if one's ladder has been up against a wall and now, no ladder, no wall. Things are simpler. "Not concerned with yesterday's state, comparing to today. You are alive now."

Awareness intensifies. "There begins to be a preference for consciousness."

Arrival, Sunday Evening

In the dining hall, people sit on cushions on the floor. Michel says, "So glad to see so many of my friends." His gracious welcome relieves some of the tension and uncertainty. He says, "Think why you have come."

There is the impression that he is attuned to something. His presence compels a silence filled with active listening. And what he is attuned to, one also can be. "Consciousness is contagious. Consciousness calls consciousness."

In this moment, one remembers why one has come.

To wake up. To feel the need to wake up. To understand in oneself what it is to wake up so one can find that again.

Understanding has appeared not because of the mind's processing information or issuing instructions. Michel's interior alignment is "contagious": one is simply with him in a flow.

Monday

    7:00 A.M. Sticks clack-clacking: time to rise.
    7:30. A bell rings. The sitting. Shoes are slipped off at the door; people sit cross-legged on cushions. With a few words, Michel guides one more deeply inside. After thirty minutes, the sitting ends. "Perhaps can carry this into the next moment."

    At breakfast, Michel says, "Meditation is only a preparation. The highest is action."

    The dining hall curtains are open revealing an enormous window-wall. Outside, only clouds. A chalet in the clouds. Little bowls of muesli and large bowls of coffee. Aware of lifting the spoon, the clinking of bowls, the weight of the coffee pot as it is handed down the rows, and very little talking. One is not quite oneself, not quite at ease but "at-tension," reigned in for the sake of remembering to stay present.

Michel speaks about "blind obedience to surface functioning."

Until now, to wake up meant to go against one's automatism by developing attention as if it were a muscle needing exercise. But now, Michel proposes something radically different, unheard of:

"It is not that attention needs to grow. The stream of Attention is there. Be touched by it, link with it, something real in you. Not ideas, thoughts, techniques, not the head, but that touch."

A stream of attention one taps into? Always there?

"It is very near but we are far away."

All morning, the tap tap tapping on stone. The hourly ringing of the bell from the church in the village—but one does not hear it every time. Coffee break at 11, lunch at 2. Michel raises his glass of water, and everyone does, too, and sips. The meal begins. A question, and Michel responds, "It is like the stone. Tap tap tap, and the stone changes. And I change, too."

∼

How many taps does it take?

And how big a hammer?

Certainly change does not happen through sitting passively at someone's feet waiting for him to give one something. Those who have come with that expectation of the oral transmission will be disappointed—as are those in search of a new way of thinking. During lunch, the man at Michel's right remarks, "The only role the mind has to play is to leave the room."

Intellect is fine, one hears, except that it *cannot change one's state*. What can?

Seeing. It "gives" a "state of freedom." Is it about cultivating a neutral witness in oneself? Or something more?

"There is an ascending movement toward a sensitivity, a receptivity," says Michel. "*Seeing* allows this other energy to appear so I can be related to it."

It is not about *what* is seen—not more information-gathering—but the emergence of "a Look upon oneself" that is like the sun coming out. Michel says, "Stay just exactly as I am. There is an Intelligence in me that can accept. Like the sun. It doesn't care if an ant is crawling across the rug. The sun radiates with life."

When one is under this Look, there is no instructing oneself to accept what is observed— no steeling oneself to something undesirable—

because acceptance is *in the very nature* of the energy present: "Acceptance is 'energetical.' Not that 'I' accept but that I am related to this energy that accepts all." To change what is seen has no appeal for it is not where the treasure lies. Indeed, it "doesn't matter what is seen; you are more awake, in this finer energy." One wishes only to stay with the flow of Attention because, like the sun, "it warms you no matter how you are, doesn't care how you are."

As one listens to Michel's voice, a shift occurs. A moment ago, one was trying to understand. Now interest shifts to what is animating one's body sitting here, and tuning to that.

Never mind images of oneself, how one *should* be: "Just let it be as it is and observe."

After hearing these words, for the next hour, one opens repeatedly to *being seen*—"seeing when mind takes over or feelings take over"—so one can return to this new receiving mode. There is a standing firm in awareness: what goes on does not take away the sense, above all, of being filled each instant with attention. The afternoon feels different. Walking down steps. Speaking with a friend. Reading a book. All accompanied by "a Look upon me, not from my ordinary self, but from That which sees objectively as it is."

The biggest surprise comes when a reactive remark pops out of one's mouth all on its own: what a reminder to wake up!

At sunset, the last rays tinge the clouds pink. The Matterhorn looks like the Sphinx. There is the sound of rushing water from a nearby stream one hears but cannot see—and a Life, palpably there, flowing through one's body.

Tuesday

6:00 A.M. The sticks. Early.
6:30. The bell rings. People file into the hall for the sitting. A pair of legs come down from the rafters. Some coughing, adjusting on one's cushion. Finally, the room is still. "I look at myself and the world, and I see that it is ordinary. I renounce this look for another."

After the sitting, one walks outside. The sun is shining. A bird flying. Sensitive ears in the silence.
At breakfast, a theme is proposed for investigation. The gist of it: there are many laws of the

universe that govern the way things are. How is it that human beings forget the dimension of consciousness and remain "unachieved"?

That is, "Is there a Law of Forgetfulness?" Does one live under it?

How to carry the question and not forget it?

"Attention is not free—taken mostly by thoughts."

The buzz of insects in the meadow grass. Michel is not at lunch. Everyone seems ordinary. Loud. Nobody mentions the theme. Something slips away.

"Accept the oscillations of consciousness and continue to attend to presence."

In the kitchen, Michel cooks up a drama, scolding all those within earshot because something is missing from the walk-in fridge and only the person in charge is allowed to take things from there. It is painful to watch yet odd because surely he is not doing this to be mean. The room is energized—no one can find the missing tray—and the women are upset. Can one remember to be present to oneself in the midst of such trying circumstances? Because it is not about the tray.

Reactive, groping—how one must look during these first few days. There's a leak somewhere: no matter how much the infinite ocean of energy pours in, none is embodied for long. Mind turning, emotions churning, one can't quite hold the charge.

Outside, the men digging a foundation look weary from a second full day's unaccustomed hard labor at high altitude. Yet some volunteer for the most strenuous jobs to find themselves at day's end just plain too tired to think. Have they discovered a way to break the hold of the ever-busy mind?

By evening, a few people are in difficulty; women in tears; men with sore backs. Frustration. Self-pity. *Everyone gets it but (poor) me.* Irritable retorts. *I don't have the time now to show you where everything goes.* A person's passive-aggressive remark snags one unawares, prompts an angry reaction—everything amplified in this atmosphere. Just when one imagines one is immune to the old miseries, galoshes go deep in the mud. "It's like a string is cut. I fall down." Vent. Brood. Plot. Wake up now? Where's the toolbox? What's the tool?

Something inside rebels. Skip the class of

sacred dances to take a shower.

It is not others' acting-out but one's own that one must "suffer"—allow—to be seen. Somebody "steps on your corns, and suddenly this reaction pours out of you. But one can have a Look upon oneself, even for a few minutes. If you prefer that Look no matter what is taking place, something will calm down in you, and you will be able to become stable in this attention—to die to those parts that keep you a slave."

No way to fix things; let the tears come; *under that Look*.

"Not to run away. To let the impressions come in. It is possible precisely when I can not. I can not, and I become so poor, so receptive. And so it is received. The attention can flow down, fill me, so there is nothing else but to *be*."

All of a sudden, it is not about one's little pain but the other person's pain behind the behavior, the world's pain, so much unconscious suffering like this in the world—

"Sadness, perhaps, which arises. See this suffering—me—others. Yet healing takes place from this energy when I'm in relation with it."

"The only way out is up."

∽

At a small group meeting in the cave-like room under the chalet, Michel sits between a man and woman visiting from the Gurdjieff institute in Paris.

Someone speaks. "I had an experience earlier today but…."

The woman to Michel's right interrupts, in her tentative English, "It is a negative to you to analyze yourself like that—'I am such and such.' Harms you. It is gossip."

Heart pounds wildly at the thought of trying to speak from presence and putting one's hands all over it. The moment passes. The room feels confined except for the small square of light from the open doorway. Staying so still in that close space, and the body tired, one fights not to doze off—presses thumbnail hard into palm—but then one hears,

"Can I liberate myself from all the illusory thoughts? For this I need free attention. To feel the call. To join with that which is always within me. It is always there—doesn't need energy, doesn't take energy. But when I am joined with it, great energy enlivens me."

Michel's voice, from another level. The feelings are touched; one is suddenly alert, all there. With the flood of feeling, tiredness evaporates. The mind quiets, reactions too, because now there appears something much more compelling:

"a subtle energy" here in oneself. And this is all that is wanted. *Yes, just this*.

One emerges from the cave aware.

After dinner, the discussion is all about ego, *what one always protects in every situation*. One has been "coarse," has "betrayed" something. "So now, to recognize that, to see…. With seeing, I can begin to allow what's good for the whole, not just one part."

The atmosphere is subdued. One is feeling remorse for the day's cavalier attitude, and it fuels a fresh resolve to begin again, new.

Wednesday

Difficulty lets go its hold. More and more, one appears in oneself and can stay. "Perhaps it takes thirty minutes, perhaps five minutes, sometimes, perhaps five seconds. The whole of me becomes sensitive to this Intelligence, this central attention, listening for it."

It is not just about "*my* attention, *put* it there," Michel says. "Let go of old ideas, years and years of them. Now that there is contact with this finer energy, a living in it—must let go of all the old ideas, not go round and round in the same circles."

But ideas draw one to a path; one loves to read, listen, be inspired. Ideas are like the glittering marquee that brings one to the door.

Yet one must go through the doorway. And for this, Michel warns, "In life there are many kinds of bait. The ideas are a kind of bait—from a loving source—for a purpose. Don't identify with the bait."

I am a seeker of truth. I am a teacher of spiritual ideas. I am a follower of important ideas that belong to me. My ideas are better than your ideas. This "I" that "thinks, believes, feels this or that"—

"All identification," says Michel.

When one's identity and self-image are bound up in some particular thing—anything transient—one has lost the connection with "this quality of energy that is not mine but what I am."

Fathoming a system of ideas may be necessary to hold one's interest over time, long enough perhaps for something of an entirely different nature to appear, "but now, when there is this central attention, an awareness of this energy, nothing else comes ahead of it, not ideas, not instructions."

Michel articulates precisely where one is in this process of finding a new center of gravity in attention. "For many years we try methods, but then, at moments, there is enough energy for a sensitivity to appear and then for this Intelligence to appear. It's not the methods that produce it. It's letting everything be, inside, just as it is, and opening to the attention."

As a support during the morning, a bell is rung every hour. A call. To go deeper into presence, or to return to it.

As one stands at the sink, thoughts are a-thinking when—instantly—one sees the water's flow, feels it on one's skin, sees how one's hands move, and the water marks on the faucet—

"The Now—not a time but a place," the axis of attention in oneself.

Can one go beyond one's limits? "The attention is not yet pure to be completely aligned with this energy—no thoughts—needs the silence. Other vibrations are there perhaps, yet just to be attracted, so at moments," (here, starting from just above the forehead, Michel's hand moves down a few inches as if pulling a thread) "to be one with this pure Attention."

Now, like this, the gesture says.

Recognize this unknown force appearing.

"What you wish for is here, now."

"We are sneakers of truth," Michel puns at dinner.

A bedtime sitting. Midnight. Can one even sit with one's back unsupported after the long day?

But the body is serving something and, surprisingly, can.

Thursday

A stirring in the pine boughs. Half the camp leaves before sunrise to drive to the Weisshorn for a hike. From the peak: mountains swathed in snowfields; the high lake shining. Being alive in this way is a joy.

In the car, exuberant from the heights, like a kid out of school, one prods the driver, "Let's go back a different way." What one doesn't know (let alone consider) is that those left behind at the chalet are preparing a special lunch. It has to be put on hold until everyone returns—and one's car is an hour late. The extravagant buffet set out on the terrace has to be carried all the way up the hill, back to the kitchen, so the food doesn't spoil in the sun.

Upon arrival, one watches from a distance as the driver is scolded: "Where have you been? Why are you so late?"

Walk quickly to the dorm and hide. A work one loves, bigger than one knows, and it all comes down to this? "Who is looking at it? If there's a show, we don't have to go to the movies!"

At lunch, Michel responds to the hikers' comments: "Being with the greatness of nature, another quality appears, another self, connected to something outside time and space. The feeling of joy when awake in this energy is natural, because suddenly you are part; you have your place in it."

A few who did not go on the trip grumble. Michel says, "It is good to feel dissatisfaction that I don't correspond to this finer energy. That comes from an intelligence. At the moment I see my inadequacy, something can open."

Can one forge a link between one's passivity and waking up? Finally, all one's beauties may be useful for something! To prompt one to look. To come under the Look that activates attention. It is a practice. This impulse: "Am I only that?" What more is here, too? "What is this reaction? Is it important? And perhaps I see that it is nothing—fear of this or wishing for that.

"But the primary thing is this relation with an energy."

∽

Asked a question about teachers, the man from Paris responds, "Yes, some are companions on a road. But if you think you have a teacher, it is a fantasy. The Teaching comes from within."

Here is a new understanding. The time comes when it is no longer about relying on teachers but about recognizing the teacher—the finer energy—in oneself.

And one is grateful, for here is "a truth felt in oneself," here is "freedom in a moment, freedom from fear and being anxious, freedom to be just as I am, giving all to what is number one in me. The central attention is there, does not wish to go into automatic behavior."

Michel says, "Something goes and returns; that's the way it is," but "another person who has this pure Attention can help me." Whoever is truly awake at a given moment is a channel through which higher consciousness appears on earth—and one "aligns irresistibly."

When speaker and listener are imbued with Attention, there is awakening mutually transmitted and received.

"With true transmission, the exchange flows in both directions. If one way only, dependence appears—on memories, associations—rather than this mutually freer state."

Friday

Walking to the sitting in a light rain. Now at week's end, it is not that one tries to wake up but that the least minute one is quiet, looking out at the mountains, the glow of presence is there. No effort needed but the noticing of it.

Listen to the rain and *be*.

Peeling forty kilos of potatoes and carrots on the porch. "There may be some busyness in the mind; let it be. I know better now where to retire from that more and more."

The movement of the hand with the peeler, so precise. *How well the body works when there is less daydreaming.* And with that thought—

There is the danger of slipping into a dream of being awake.

"I don't know who I am but I am full of dreams—dreams of work, even."

On the hillside, a man with a wheelbarrow goes up and down.

Just when one gets comfortable in heaven, one pontificates at a meeting in that all-too-earnest tone one hears in others (not Michel) but never in oneself. Michel's comment on the topic oh so gently pricks one's ego, triggering internal dialogue—*I didn't do well, they don't appreciate me.* Will it take over? For a minute, an hour, or all year? One forgets the Famous Energy and that "you don't have to be a certain way to be related to this energy." One scrambles to recover.

But self-justification is a longtime favorite dish. One indulges for half an hour—instant replay—what one really meant to say, what one should have said. Even as it continues, it "feels pornographic," that is, "not fitting for what you have tasted—see that—go toward the best. Respect one's nature."

Michel has shown one something—so dramatically—

You are not what you think.

Here is a test of one's work: to "suffer" one's arrogance, welcoming the Look that lets it be. Exposed, ego acting up, and at the same time—one realizes—*something here that isn't hurt at all.* One feels troubled by the poorness of one's favorite dish (and the smell), but what is momentous is that seeing is here, too, *and one knows it.*

"When you are dispersed, let the attention touch your state as it is. See the power you have in you."

One is only halfway up the mountain.

More than that:
"You still believe in the one who thinks she knows. You think it is yours, this experience. Like this little bit of carpet that needs to have a speck taken off. You still think it belongs to you.
"*There is no you.*
"It is complete identification. Either one is identified with the body or one is in this flow, the true Self."

There is no you.

At any other time, the statement would make no sense, but in a long mutual moment looking into Michel's eyes, one feels it is true.

Saturday

A day of contemplation. To look at one's life, what one receives, what one can give. "Stay in concentration, not go far away from myself but to let this flow of life penetrate me more deeply."

Clouds billow up, as grand as the peaks. The Matterhorn, bathed in light.

"Can I liberate myself from all my concerns and enter the mystery?"

At the sitting: "Now, no more pretensions. Can be simple. I see that I could not give myself totally to the experience. I feel remorse for that. Could not come totally under the influence of the Source. And today I understand that. So I can go on, simply, letting this force, this influence, work in me. Now an inner sun begins little by little to appear. And I begin to feel my responsibility. To be aligned with this energy."

"And perhaps an impulse comes to go out into life in a meaningful way."

How to help others and the world? As one sits with the mountains, *service* takes on new meaning.

At any moment, what is being served? "Look at how your day was—when you were aggressive with people." One regrets the way one treats others, thinks about others. But trying to hold onto this new expansive feeling or to behave in a certain way in the future—fix oneself—is just old-mind's imaginary notion about change. "Not to manipulate, but to *see*"—one understands this better now—so attention appears, "and then all of me serves that, obeys that."

To be responsible, to serve—not as some grandiose idea but by being actually aware of "a flowing in of fine energy" as one sits, speaks, moves. "Being sensitive each moment to a finer quality of life, of impressions, permits you to give that, and so create another quality of circulation among us."

What to serve? "This higher Intelligence in us." At moments: "Help each other through living in this pure Attention. From it can come my best action in the world, my best action for others."

On the hillside, sunlight brushes the tops of the pines and flows in soft ripples down to the valley. From one's perch on a bench above the garden: the silence of the peaks.

"Quietness is not something I 'do.' It is the state of not being taken. Already there is a relation."

A week ago, one's spiritual life meant "something I do" to get results, but now, *doing* and *getting* recede in importance. "When we are related to this energy inside us, it is a miracle. The goodness of it pours through me and changes everything."

Michel also says, "Going away and coming back are part of the same oneness, the same process."

The thread lost? A pause. A Look upon oneself.

For what was here a moment ago is still here, always here.

"There is a Greatness. Above me. Through me. To join with it again."

At lunch, no strain, no hurry. Aware equally of a current in oneself and the one talking, smiling, eating. When one becomes "more interested in this connection with something precious," then "ego and judgment melt away. Love and compassion can come through me—compassion for my parts, too."

Compassion for my parts, too. "How can one help but love that which enters, all goodness, and wish to correspond to That?"

One may not yet be stable in this Attention—perhaps "thoughts come and take it"—but "I can return, become active, engaged, related again to that, feel gratitude, not to go far away from that. Both worlds together for a moment."

Both together, "higher" and "lower," awakening and everyday life. It is no longer a case of wanting the opposite of what one has or rejecting one for the other—that is not balance. Be in both at the same time, ordinary self and the finer energy. "Just be sure you're really letting the contact appear." Always in question: "Am I in both?"

"When I am aware of this axis in me, am there 'in the middle,' none of the forces of life can take me away."

A walk in the meadow to pick wildflowers for the evening celebration. One no longer treads a razor's edge; in this moment, one is at ease, porous, juicy.

"Quite extraordinary to receive both impressions. Heavenly energy—to live quietly in it, attend to it because it draws the attention. At the same time, to be in life, in movement, centered in this place of attention, letting all the impressions be received.

"How to be true to yourself? One would have to find the place in one where both streams coexist."

The bell rings in the church tower.
One stands like a pine in the sunlight.

∼

"Work is the moment of relation with something finer. To be related to this energy. To open directly. To be a channel for that, more and more in life."

At the dorm, women lay out their party clothes. Preparations begin in the dining hall. Rugs unroll. Golden fabric glitters on the wall. "Not to let the mind go here and there, now, out of respect for this energy, for attending to it. It is your fundamental activity."

A flurry of actors on the terrace. Musicians bring their instruments. Artists get out their paints. The choral group rehearses. Voices in harmony rise up through the chalet. "We become sensitive to a quality that dwells within us, among us."

And no one left behind.

One's relationship to others has changed. Clothes, mannerisms, speech are not one's focus—no judgments there at all. That one can be with others in this way even for a short while is a gift. In conversation, one listens with a tenderness one has not felt before. For the first time, other people's suffering is more important than one's own.

"This energy accepts all as it is. When I am accepted, I can give."

That night, in the dining hall, baskets overflow with meadow flowers. Behind Michel on the wall are four freshly painted panels of an alpine scene. A duet on the piano. Toasts of armagnac. Skits satirizing how the week went, how one sounds when talking about oneself—it is so good to laugh—

"To be fluid here, allowing each one the freedom to express what he is. You know when you are not really yourself.

"Here, just to be yourself, free, in this Attention."

How unlike the first night, one's impression of everyone this evening, laughing, participating. One does not view others through the filter of like-and-dislike but sees instead what shines there.

"Something is different. I know where I'm going. I begin to be confident in this return to awareness of this energy—the source of peace and tranquility in me."

"And so there appears a tender feeling for the world."

Departure, Sunday Morning

A breeze stirs the tips of the tall grasses. The whole world poised for a moment.

On the breakfast table, large white peaches, the perfection of ripeness, in lovely bowls. People in their traveling clothes look as if they have put on their personalities with their finery—but their essence shines through.

At breakfast, after everyone is served, the room becomes still; a natural pause; all together in a wonderful silence.

Finally, Michel says, "We almost forgot to eat!" and the meal begins.

Today, something is normal in how one feels in oneself, in how one sees others—a "normal" one has never known before. And it is the same for everyone.

Michel says, "When the attention is with this other energy permeating me—very concentrated yet very light, free, wishing nothing, needing nothing—everything takes its proper place.

"And this energy is still not the highest. This first stage is important because this force, this energy I perceive when awake, is the child of another higher energy that, perhaps, will come."

Dishes are washed and put away. A stream of people going up the footpath to the driveway. "There is joy in recognizing this action within.

Going into the silence. Recognizing this, in us, of true value."

Moving about in the world is "like riding a horse through a new country: everything is brand new. There is clarity." As one waits on line at the airport, sights and sounds come in but do not take one away: "The axis of attention can stay by itself even, because it is fed by every impression."

The usual me takes part in the world from a place of well-being when "this Attention is first":

"Nothing which I call 'me'—thoughts, feelings, reactions—is mine. Not one thing. Yes, I can witness my functions, but nothing belongs to me.

"Let everything go.

"Recognize this Intelligence appearing. It knows better than you. Receive it. Join it. Respect it.

"Nothing belongs to me except that which recognizes my true nature. When I can see this, it is a great liberation. And I come to live under a new influence."

When one perceives the stream of life energy, it can flow through oneself more and more, says Michel. "Then it can have an action in the world."

And this is what is needed, what I am here for.

WEEK ONE

Monday

Everything We Need Is Here in Us

Perhaps there is no inclination to turn inward. Let it be. Just watch. The power of attention more and more can fill the body. The greatest need we have is to know who I am, and I can know that only by this energy incarnating the body.

Everything we need is here in us. Everything for fuller being. There is a kind of sacred descent of attention that can bring this about. Seeing the obstacles, thoughts, feelings, yes, perhaps a pressure that keeps me from it. But if I can relax inside, just allow the pure attention to flow in, be in that. Very natural. It's what we are.

Attention: a sacred energy coming into me. Be sensitive to it. Recognize again and again that it is there.

To Let the Experience Open

To let the experience open—not to be too quick to have ideas about it. Situate yourself in this calm, empty space.

Know in your body what it is to be present so you can find it again.

For many years we try methods, but then, at moments, there is enough energy for a sensitivity to appear and then for this Intelligence to appear. It is not the methods that produce it. It's letting everything be, inside, just as it is, and opening to the attention.

The stronger the attention, the lighter the body. Very pleasant—yes—but not to be taken by this lightness. The attention is coming first, the body second.

Pushes and pulls here and there maybe, but I am so attracted to be joined with this energy, there is nothing else as important. That is how it feels.

Sensation as a Ground so
Attention Can Stay

Attention is what relates the higher and lower. But it is not free—taken mostly by thoughts. It needs a ground: the body.

"Sensation"—always the result of the meeting of two forces. Sensation is the experience of contact between attention and body, not for itself, but as a ground so the attention can stay.

A living axis in me, among the myriad of movements.

I can be sensitive to them, sensitive to breathing.

And a feeling arises of body, mind, and soul here together.

How important breathing is. It helps you join the axis. To have a direct experience of all of myself, a central attention.

Participating in a movement greater than ourselves, of which all of this is part.

Completely relaxed….

Something fine can fill me.

And I am sure it is there, this energy. I am aligned with it. There is a conviction that it is there. Like the fisherman who knows the fish is in the pond. And not only conviction but also attraction. All my functions go to it willingly.

When this energy is there and I am sure of it, aware of it moment by moment, I begin to *be*.

Free Attention—Not Taken by Anything

Searching for consciousness—that is the essential. You are too much concentrated on yourself. Searching for consciousness, sensitive, receiving with an attention more and more free, more and more pure.

And when this central Intelligence appears, to respect it, more and more. Not to betray it.

It is very near, but we are far away.

To realize, with remorse, that I have been coarse, have betrayed it. So now, to recognize that, to see.

Attention is the only matter that can receive finer influences. Free attention—not taken by anything. If taken, it means I am concentrated on me, my functions, a thought, a feeling, a reaction. Free attention: an attention that is free of the vibrations on the surface.

So remember this other mode of being, more sensitive, just receiving. Without the presence of

I, of Self, all the efforts are nothing. You must remember the Self, allow it to be. You must respect it. What you do not respect, vanishes.

Again and again, to remember the Self, letting it be received with a free attention, penetrating more deeply. Come back to it—not to go a long period any day without that.

Tuesday

Correspond to This Sacred Attention

Everything begins with the impression of myself. Not some theoretical idea about sincerity, but deep questioning. Can I come to this evidence?

How can one help but love that which enters, all goodness, and wish to correspond to That?

See how to correspond to this sacred Attention coming into me. When I am related to this Intelligence, respect it as the representative of the sacred, from the Source; then it can have an action in the world.

Then I'm not thinking about me but can listen, can receive impressions of the other, called to stand in the place that can receive impressions. Not psychological—not thinking about it, imagination about it.

This Attention is *in* the body and *beyond* the body. "You" cannot "do" it—fortunately. But recognizing this Intelligence, you can correspond to it, and then join it, irresistibly.

Whatever Comes, I Am Free

Seeing comes from Above. There is an energy I can be related to. As human beings, we have the capacity for another dimension to appear simultaneously with all this that thinks, feels, reacts. When I am focused in seeing, this other can be as it is, and whatever comes and goes, I am free.

The more I stay, the more I can stay.

I have a sense, then, of the meaning of life, and there is joy in that. When this seeing is primary, there is no mental manipulation. There is another quality present that attracts me.

To be very light, and objective, not reacting, not judging.

And then the question deepens: Who am I? Related to this influence, for us, a new world opens.

Concentrating Requires Determination

What is concentration?

It is a returning of forces. A focusing on presence. A centering of energies. Even when tired, dispersed, already just to feel far away from that allows some light to enter.

A sensing exercise is something sacred, from a mysterious origin above me, to bring down into me a finer energy, help me join with it. Always to treat with respect this energy that is not from me but in me, that I can perceive.

Create a space—fill more and more, until you feel something: *I AM.*

Concentrating oneself requires determination. So then this other energy can appear. It is a great relief!

When you are dispersed, let the attention touch your state as it is. Just be sure you're really letting the contact appear. See the power you have in you.

With concentration comes purification of the attention so it remains free from the movement of all the energies around, until finally, it is free to receive all the impressions of *what is.*

Through me, impressions can go toward quite an unexpected Intelligence that we receive.

Wednesday

One Can Have a Look Upon Oneself

Working with others: it is the opportunity to see myself. To see when I am related to an energy and when perhaps there is a little tension around it, and all the things that come from self-image, from what I think others want from me, how I want them to see me, what I believe myself to be—the fears, wish for control, wish them to be different, me to be different. We are all like this. We want to be somebody when, really, we could be so free.

Even passing a stranger in the street, you see that there are tensions. He steps on your corns, and suddenly this reaction pours out of you. We are all carrying this around all the time—this poisonous material, so-called negative emotions—it is in us, cannot be different. But one can have a Look upon oneself, to stay with that, even for a few minutes.

If you keep looking, prefer that Look upon you no matter what is taking place, something will calm down in you, and you will be able to become stable in this attention—to die to those parts that keep you a slave—and a new freedom and possibility will appear.

And the mark of this is that for even a short while you feel related to the world, everything and everyone.

Let Go of Ideas

Being awake in this finer energy is like being in the shower. Either you're in it or not. "In it" feels completely different. Bathe in it, with all of you.

And when you're not in it, it's not a question of being a policeman, but more of abandonment of what's not necessary. What is really needed?

Like a pianist—he just listens—hears what is not needed, abandons that, and the music becomes purer.

We are more spontaneous, natural human beings when "in the shower." Integrated. No separation, no trying, no doing, open to others.

And not just to be in the shower but to let go of old ideas, years and years of them.

Now that there is contact with this finer energy, a conviction of it, a living in it—must let go of all the old ideas, not go round and round in the same circles.

Abandon what is not necessary.

Not to manipulate, but to see. Give all the attention to receiving this energy.

Everything in life is in waves, up and down, and so with presence. Remain open and attentive, and it will find you. It needs you.

Consciousness Is Contagious

We begin to understand how to come to something in ourselves, but we do not yet know how to work with others.

Try first with nature, then with animals, then with children. Then with near ones to you, then with the baker, then with… [*smiles, indicating everyone here*].

To recognize the reality of this person, for instance. To recognize her as an animated being. Then we can have a relation with that person that is unexpected.

Work should bring unity, not separation.

Another person who has this pure Attention can help me in a moment.

To be fluid here, allowing each one the freedom to express what he is. You know when you are not really yourself.

Here, just to be yourself, free, in this Attention. Work with others is so much more powerful—the atmosphere helps me—can do so much more. Need for something to pass, to circulate.

Consciousness is contagious. Consciousness calls consciousness.

Thursday

We Are Reminders for Each Other

We can strengthen this current we are aware of. Impressions of life can be food for consciousness. Who is here receiving?

Why do we need sometimes to come together like this with others? Because together we can begin to understand something. Because we are reminders for each other to come to myself. We need others, humankind, as mirrors to know who we are.

And the greatest reminding factor is remorse. This part wants this, feels this, thinks that—discomfort. I realize I have betrayed something. This is the beginning of a feeling of remorse.

Remorse—like lightning. There is no judgment in remorse. I realize I am far away, and I come back to receiving—to the Self. With seeing, I can begin to allow what's good for the whole, not just one part. Feel universal forces. Discover that which is most precious, just beneath the surface of the mirror.

Today, not worrying about how others see me, not beliefs. Just re-centering. How to participate with others while in this world?

How to begin, sensitive, in each moment?

If we could see how to start all the time, it would be a very great thing.

To Be with This Other Person

To be with this other person who is difficult to listen to—yet to be free in the attention, just letting him be.

Suffering occurs when we try to get him to be this way or that.

When you are working, a feeling arises of being open to others, letting them be, letting me be—and still related to this energy. No more pretending. You need the taste of this even if only for a few moments.

When you dislike or envy someone, you must come to yourself, come into presence, to be just. Come back to a sensitivity.

You can join this vibration so it can penetrate deeper, not be stopped. We are the creator of obstacles [*smiles*].

This is the challenge. When it is impossible, that is precisely when the Self can be remembered.

Ask yourself, "Like this, is this all there is?"

What could prepare me for right thinking? You harvest what you seed.

I Begin To Feel My Responsibility

I begin to feel my responsibility. To be aligned with this energy brings consciousness, love, and will. My responsibility: to align.

Thinking stops it.

When younger, perhaps, had to try this and that, but now, when there is this central attention, an awareness of this energy, nothing else comes ahead of it, not ideas, not instructions.

The first initiation is recognition of and respect for Attention, its freedom and independence. And an attraction toward it. Respect that it comes from a very high source.

Let it be; turn inward. To an unknown reality. This Attention is a sacred thing.

Let's try to live this together today, to work together, to serve—what? A mystery. Beyond form. To accomplish something together, not knowing what.

Friday

Absolutely Objective, Like the Sun

Sometimes we are threatened, and it is then that we appear. Or I wish to have compassion—but it isn't me that can have compassion; it is this Intelligence in me that can have compassion. I see my friend acting this way and that, but I observe, open, so "The Boss" appears, this sacred Attention, and then all of me serves that, obeys that.

It is objective, absolutely objective, this Attention. Like the sun. It warms you no matter how you are, doesn't care how you are.

Also to feel remorse when you know you are separated from it—but to stay with that. To realize that *going away* and *coming back* are part of the same oneness, the same process.

I must be sensitive to my state every moment. So the attention comes. But we commit the sin of wanting to change according to some idea, even an idea about a past experience. I have images of myself, how I should be.

We are addicted to beliefs. Our strongest addiction. It takes subtle forms, this veil of idiocy. But faith—that is another story. A certitude that is beyond mind functioning. Very different.

Why is it difficult sometimes to listen to other people's words about work? That is because you still believe in the one who thinks she knows. You think it is yours, this experience. Like this little bit of carpet that needs to have a speck taken off. You still think it belongs to you.

There is no you.

It is complete identification.

Either one is identified with the body or one is in this flow, the true Self.

Recognize These Two Worlds

To recognize something that was unknown but is now immediate, unique—because it is everywhere. This is an exercise that is needed because one is not seeing what is, and one suffers from that.

To recognize the higher and the lower creates a feeling. Let these forces enter and do what they need to do. Otherwise they just act through me but don't transform me, which can take place only through recognition of their essential qualities. Each day, have a representation of something we wish to recognize—without defense mechanisms, without all this other, just what is inside. No more mind. No more method. The higher and the lower can be related through me.

And I see that breathing is a sacred thing, relating these....

Breathe in... no tension....
Breathe out... no tension....
Breathe in... toward the higher....
Breathe out... toward the lower....

This axis of attention can be a channel that relates the two worlds.

There can be a progressive recognition of the two worlds through a sensitivity.

The more I recognize these two worlds, the more the feeling can appear which relates them. Always the question, *Am I in both?*

With a Very Active Attention

With a very active attention, I can receive this energy. Not that "I do it" but that even despite my effort, help is given.

When very quiet inside—need an atmosphere of sensitivity—aware of breathing—become more interested in that, in this connection with something precious, so ego and vanity and judgment melt away.

I don't want to lose that because it's precious, so I return, not to grasp at it—not imagination and thought—but a very active attention.

"I" can't love, but when my parts are related, in balance, equilibrium, the two worlds co-exist.

Love and compassion can come through me—compassion for my parts, too.

Then thoughts come and take it, but I can return, become active, engaged, related again to that, feel gratitude, loving to serve that more and more, not to go far away from that. To be able to experience something real; to receive from Above this that is real—a movement—both worlds together for a moment.

Saturday

Suddenly, This Contact with A Higher Energy

There is joy in recognizing this action within. Going into the silence. Recognizing this, in us, of true value. Suddenly you see this contact with a higher energy that creates more and more a feeling of belonging, of being part of that. You don't have a separation.

To try with your family, too. Maybe some are dreaming, some are running away, but you are sensitive; this Intelligence appears, even if only for five minutes. It may be five minutes that no one forgets.

Picture your life from birth. Take half an hour to think of father, then mother, child, sister, brother. Feel the relatedness. Repair the past.

And perhaps an impulse comes to go out into life in a meaningful way.

What Comes First Is Attention

More and more, what comes first is this Attention.

The body, really, is second. It is not the body that is important but the atmosphere around it. The atmosphere becomes permeated with this finer vibration, in the stillness.

Because of a word, an image, a sensation, I think I know the body. I do not know what the body is. No longer pretending to know… and it relaxes…. And another quality is there.

The body likes to have a "boss." Not the usual boss. The attention lets the body be seen.

An axis begins to appear, of pure attention.

Keep something of this inner secret life alive while in activity in the world. A kind of asceticism.

Personality is like a coat. It may be beautiful, I need it, but it is just a coat I can put on, like playing a role.

When there is an inner intensity, it is like a doctor stitching a wound. The attention is called to each stitch, and there is no room for personality to take over.

The essence and personality are one: impressions can flow through both, bring life. Like having a boss, personality under the influence of essence. There is a sensitivity. This atmosphere, filled with energy. The body, like an envelope.

Respect this atmosphere, this energy contained in the body. Feel responsible for it….

Thinking breaks the charm.

This Intelligence That Is Not Mine

This Intelligence that is not mine—I respect this central attention, love this attention, so everything serves it. The cosmos works this way, too—like us—in service to this energy.

Retaste, retaste, retaste this center into which everything comes.

Have faith in consciousness. Faith, like love, is a relationship between two energies: the higher and the intelligence that receives it.

Permanence is not a quality of the manifest world but of the Unmanifest that no one can see but which rules everything.

There is a Greatness. Above me. Through me. To join with it again.

What Is Still Is the Attention

Stillness: what is still is the attention.

This axis of attention—all life flowing through me.

Let the impression go in deeper. Not so much on the surface.

Even in the stillness… I *think*. But now there is enough sensitivity to see that the word, the idea, is not the real thing.

It is important to love this energy, respect this energy coming through you from Above.

And then, even subtler energies can come into you—the Light can come into you.

Today, to be peaceful. Quiet mind. No agitation. Just receiving impressions. Let them come in.

Life can be distressing, but the light of consciousness can be in me.

All my thoughts, feelings, ideas are nothing compared to this precious treasure, this quality of energy that is not mine but what I am.

Perhaps can carry this into the next moment.

Sunday

What Is the Change in Us?

What is the change in us from how we were when we arrived? More collected, yes, and the body is second, not first. It has its needs, ego too, but all of it submits naturally to this higher force. It is that which is felt to come first.

All these forces in me that usually have their way in my ordinary state because there is no higher force there—now all are drawn up in the current.

Ego, features, are still there, but now they serve. And when they serve the higher force, all is changed.

We see how we are, how in a moment we are radically changed and understand something, and in the next, we are back as we were. I can be tolerant of the moods, features, of others knowing how it is with me. One moment, all serves the higher. Another moment—without the higher there to draw to itself those currents—other things take over.

More and more, with attending to presence, allowing higher forces to enter, staying collected, returning, we can live in a new way.

Even when you are not feeling well, you have a special opportunity because you see you do not want to spend your energy any old way. You can serve this energy. And the energy can heal.

From it can come my best action in the world, my best action for others. Help each other through living in this pure Attention.

An Inner Sun Begins To Appear

Here I have been worked upon by conditions.
Now, no more pretensions. Can be simple. I see
that I could not give myself totally to the
experience. I feel remorse for that. I could not
come totally under the influence of the Source.
And today, I understand that.

So I can go on, simply, letting this force, this
influence, work in me. I can be confident now
because this understanding is based on facts.

Now an inner sun begins little by little to appear.
Can radiate.

Bringing lightness of body and clarity of mind.
Bringing light to every cell.

And I begin to feel my responsibility.
To be aligned with this energy.

Work out of respect for the Source. It is not the
experience or the result of this relation with the
energy that matters but the relation with its Source.

Letting Impressions Be Received

There is a heavenly quality, a finer vibration, freeing. There is also an earthly quality that can be received.

Quite extraordinary to receive both impressions. Heavenly energy—to live quietly in it, attend to it because it draws the attention. At the same time, to be in life, in movement, centered in this place of attention, letting all the impressions be received.

How to be true to yourself? One would have to find the place in one where both streams coexist.

Here we can try to be real human beings. A real human being is one who is connected to heaven and earth. There are the three elements: heaven, earth, and the human community.

How to be in life, in yourself, living in all the levels, without being artificial? How, in ordinary life, to live in all three worlds? Because if I'm not aware of living in all the worlds, I am nothing.

The first responsibility is to join with this place, this central attention. Can only do this alone. Solitary. But when joined with it, quite a different view—do not feel alone. Can go out in the world.

The subjective tempo is returning. At the same time, moments of being more conscious. Not to go out to the object—a sound, a thought, a movement—but the impression can be *received.*

Sensitivity Everywhere

It's a question of which influence I'm under.

You receive impressions according to your state. When I'm here, it means there's a silence.

A central attention appears, free of all different kinds of vibrations occurring. So "self-observation" comes to have a very different meaning: observation by the Self, from Above.

We are in a process to come under another influence. There is "my" attention, secondary attention, that runs up the mountain, sees obstacles, does this or that. But when the central attention is there, we cross the threshold for a moment. This Attention is first.

Perhaps it takes thirty minutes, perhaps five minutes, sometimes, perhaps five seconds. The whole of me becomes sensitive to this Intelligence, this central attention, listening for it. We were made for it.

Sensitivity everywhere. Nothing but sensitivity….

A kind of whole-hearted emptiness. A trusting emptiness.

So that a finer influence can act on me, in the silence.

And even despite myself, I begin to receive it, yield to it, a channel for it.

And perhaps a threshold is reached when I belong to That.

WEEK TWO

Monday

Acceptance Is "Energetical"

Stay just exactly as I am. There is an Intelligence in me that can accept. Like the sun. It doesn't care if an ant is crawling across the rug. The sun radiates with life.

This acceptance is not psychological; it's "energetical." It's not something I can "do." But this finer energy can.

Like water through rocks, penetrating, irrigating every cell, from the relation with this energy. I need to be touched more by this, worked by this, in the cells. Then love, will, and consciousness can begin to live.

Acceptance as we talk of it now is only preliminary psychological acceptance. It's okay, but when the real thing appears, this higher energy, we are completely transformed in a moment.

This energy accepts all as it is. All the functions are put in order under the Master.

The more one lives in this energy, the more clarity one has. Can see things. You must recognize this central core, this presence, this Self in you, more and more, to let it come. In this contact, an energy is formed that relates me to a living world.

When I am accepted, I can give.

Join This Attention

Even a little bit of conscious energy is like gold from which something can start. I acknowledge this during the day.

When there is attention, the body is light. Not brutal in action, speech.

Instead of my mind-dominated usual condition, my wavering state, I join this Attention. When there is a shift in my center of gravity to this Attention, I do not judge the other but have a preference for this. Which is more real? All parts become balanced, and something refined can permeate. Quiet inside. Sensitivity appears naturally.

Not pretend. Not "do." But become aware of myself for the first time.

Now is the first time. Sensitive. Living in this Attention. Join this Attention, the gold from which something can start.

The Moment of Relation with
Something Finer

Ask something of myself. Ask myself to allow the body to be seen. Return. Be in relation. Body is secondary; this relationship is primary.

Effort—preliminary—creates a substance that allows you to receive something very fine. Work is the moment of relation with that something finer. Total sensitivity. Total receptivity.

Concern should be with my parts' not knowing how to allow that to be—I'm not educated. I need the shock of a moment of realizing incapacity, but now, go deeply "innerly."

Watchfulness—feel a responsibility for that. The more conscious you are of what takes place, the more it takes place.

This Touch of Energy

Quietness is not something I "do." It is the state of not being taken. Already there is a relation.

Quiet comes from Above. I can't make myself quiet. But when sensitive, that the sun is behind the cloud, listen, come inside. Become a purified channel for this energy from just Above. Let it be received.

Everyone can be a channel for higher energy. In working, we purify the channel, and then the energy comes through. It is a taste of freedom—no mind—and when you are connected with that, you don't have to pretend.

It is not that attention needs to grow. The stream of Attention is there. Be touched by it, link with it, something real in you. To be responsible for that. Not ideas, thoughts, techniques, not the head, but that touch. Being in the stream of Attention. To be in question every moment because there is this link; this touch appears. Let the rest go, thoughts, beliefs, comments: am I only that?

Be in question, sensitive now to the touch, what's real, the core in me. Go faithfully toward that which you know is real. Test things, be in life, but also more and more to open to impressions, to breath, to this touch of energy. Then you understand, can be yourself.

It's all unknown. The mind will never get it. Look inward. We're all designed like this. Treat it all as unknown.

Tuesday

Not To Analyze Your Functions

To work instantaneously. Not to analyze your functions, this about the mind, this about the emotions—am I this angry little man? Am I only that? To ask yourself, when you notice you are groping, you are in this or that reaction, this or that function: *Am I only that?*

When you taste a certain order in yourself, there can be more joy, more love. This is liberation from stupidity. You think you have no Master. So distracted, you think that, but if you had no Master, you wouldn't be here.

How to work? Just reduce a little the tension in you now. Then you begin to be drawn to a space within which another kind of see-er exists. To have a relationship with this see-er. Begin to receive. See what is the mind more. Embrace more.

But let's not spoil the miraculous with words. More important to perceive this quality. Then I'm not so attracted to my functions. Try to be active this morning.

Respect When the Energy Is There

This relationship "interiorly" is primary. This is where growth can appear. Otherwise I just go around and around. I'm stuck in feelings, judgments. When I am aware, energy passes, goes deeper.

Respect that moment when the energy is there—you don't care about yourself. In serving that, respecting that, caring for that, you grow. You are transformed.

Respect my nature as all nature. One can't stay up maybe, but one can become conscious of one's nature. And when one has put one's old clothes back on for a moment and it feels pornographic, not fitting, inappropriate for what you have tasted—see that—go toward the best. Respect your nature.

Keep this question alive: Can I be a little more sensitive to myself now? Can I be a little more aware of myself now? Just that. Wherever I am, however I am.

That question—that look inside—can immediately relate me to an Intelligence. A new condition appears that allows connection with this energy. Must put this first. Must respect this.

What you respect, you are attentive to.

Come Toward the Source

The more I come toward the Source, which contains everything, the more I am attracted to it. Very simple. Very direct. I may start on the surface—there are different degrees and relationships to that—but as I come inside….

Being is containing everything. Separation is suffering, separation of body, of thought, of feelings.

Some moments, very subtle in myself, even when looking at the world—this silence, this vibration. When I come closer to the center, to the Source, I begin to flow, be in that, attracted more and more.

The attention serves two masters. Either the deeper attention is there and you do just what is needed, nothing extra. Or it serves impressions mechanically and there is much more than needed, much extra, unnecessary.

This Attention can put me in contact with the sacred in me. It is a gift given to me, like my life.

Purification of attention: I can begin to listen, to *be*. To see what is, not wish for another time or state. What you wish for is here, now.

A Taste of Truthfulness

There is something above all: a taste of truthfulness. Our aim should be this Attention—our god—because it permits to see. My own attention is important but it has preferences. But this Attention has no black and white, no hopes, no despair—and helps to accept *what is.*

Misery now can become richness in a moment. And the richness now can become a misery. The Attention sees all this. The Attention sees everything more and more through you, if you can go into the silence, respect that. You know it's the truth.

How to reach this Attention? Some moments concentrated, other moments, so much joking and laughter. It is important to see what is necessary.

The calling back of the attention has an awakening power. Not to confuse the one who is aligned in this Attention with the one who *thinks.* Two different persons. So be careful, watchful. More and more to see *what is.*

And when this central Intelligence appears in you, to respect it, not to betray it. If only you knew what it is, could see what it is, you would respect it and know its worth. Not for self-glory. Not for a nice experience and then you are passive again. But as a truth felt in oneself.

Wednesday

It Is Possible Precisely When I Cannot

Not to run away. To stay with the impression, to let the impressions come in.

It is possible precisely when I cannot. I cannot… and I become so poor, so receptive…. And so it is received.

The Attention can flow down, fill me, so there is nothing else but to *be*.

In life, always in another mode, trying to do things—but I could try to *be*.

The Attention is non-judgmental. Let it touch your state. When there is an inner attention, the mind clears, just goes to what is needed. A central attention. When joined with that, no more conditioning.

Just let it be as it is and observe. Know that the reaction of the moment is fleeting. This other—the associative part—it is not you. It is interesting how you go to that small part.

Sometimes I'm like a rat. Goes to one door—shut. To another door—shut. To another door—shut. So it accepts, sits there, and begins to *be.*

What You Give Depends on
What You Receive

There is a circulation of energies. In life, it is a circulation of goods. There is a law, mathematically exact: you get what you give. In life, you receive what you give.

But here, *what you give depends on what you receive.* The quality of impressions, of beauty, of fineness, you receive. Being sensitive each moment to a finer quality of life, of impressions, permits you to give that, and so create another quality of circulation among us.

The moment when I'm fed up, have had enough, stay another few minutes and so transform this impression. I can receive but not yet give.

The only discovery is this energy. Affirmation of this energy. Be with this energy. When you are, it does not matter what is thought or felt or done because the primary perception is this energy.

First this energy animates the head—becomes active. But it does not end there. Must penetrate down. Heart, feelings, are touched. All that is personal drops away, is nothing. The possibility of something new appears.

And I can be sincere.

Contact with an Intelligence

Turning again and again—opening—to this flow can be the support for living.

Begin with a sensation of the body, then the energy in it. Work begins when there is contact with an Intelligence. The rest is preparation.

How to pass from ordinary life to this sensitivity immediately with no bridge?

Really empty. And quiet.

Let the flow of Attention permeate, animate.

Somehow—you pass. You don't know, but somehow you pass. The more contact, the more in relation to That—what's real—the more you wish to serve.

Not to go against anything, but to come toward. To concentrate, to align. Where is this Intelligence in me?

Open to it—very natural—not against mind or feelings but a sense that they are not the whole story. Intimations of another reality.

You have been in it many times.

Thursday

Authentic Self Can Emerge

To have a natural attention flowing into oneself—no exercises, no "truth." Pathways into essence so that authentic self can emerge, can *be*.

To see—to have a real impression of myself here. Very natural, this flow of attention in me. Just let it in. Stay with myself here. Be in this "middle place" where I can receive impressions.

If the impression brings me back to myself, I have received it.

If I get attached to it, I have not received it consciously.

Free attention. Sacred attention. Knowing the difference between real attention and ersatz. Coming to myself in a way that is quite natural.

What is the essence of work? When I am in the stream of sacred attention, it's not that I choose. The way is "choiceless"—just be in That. And real kindness flows.

You Are Called To Attend

You are where your attention is. All that there is at any moment is where your attention is. When experiencing this Attention that is all-embracing, if you have negative emotions, feelings, thoughts, you need not be a victim so that's all that exists.

What is effort? If the sense of the ordinary "I" disappears, that is effort.

Along the way, make efforts and understand many things. But real effort—there needs to be another word for it—is "choiceless"; it is being called; it is being in relation to something, responding by acknowledging, attending. "Choiceless" response: you are called to attend.

The germ of Reason—higher Intelligence—we have this in us. When I am in the flow of Attention, it appears; it links us with God. Can understand. Can *be.* Can let be.

What the Body Is For

We must try to live the ideas. Today there is a threat to the work. Fourth Way ideas are everywhere. They are on the supermarket shelf. So we must live the ideas.

There is one great sin I recognize: I don't see *what is.* I don't let things be, inside or outside. I need more to let things be as they are. Not to interfere.

This body is not mine. It belongs to the dweller— but it is mostly not available to the dweller so the dweller is not there. But it belongs to the dweller because only to him does it give itself completely.

My state depends on the quality of energy in the body. I can take refined energy from the air in breathing from this central attention. The dweller needs this. There is a subtle energy penetrating the body, moving through it, and I can perceive that because I am a human being.

Now I begin to recognize a higher Intelligence. An Attention, which is not mine, can be received—

received by a finer body within the physical body.

The thread of this subtle influence—recognize that, be with that. This is what the body is for. It is nothing without that.

Friday

An Energy That Permeates with Full Authority

This Attention is always there. I go away from it. This central attention behind—join with it.

There is something in you that cannot be threatened. It is always there. Come close to it—and become more yourself, more real. Order comes from that.

There is no place in us yet where *I* can stay, can abide—needs a finer body. But still, as we become quieter, steadier in attention, can taste that, can draw nearer.

And then suddenly, I am living in awareness of this finer energy, and everything is okay. I can *be.* I can be related to others.

This energy—*I*—that exists does not demand, does not ask, yet when one experiences it, one feels called; there is a demand to be with that.

When aware of this flow that permeates: What is body? What is energy?

If ordinary thoughts, feelings, body become so strong, it is either one or the other. Yet, at moments, there is an energy that permeates with full authority.

Ascent and Descent, the Same Energy

There are two movements, as spoken of by René Guénon:

Ascending... toward *I*
Descending... then manifesting through
        all you have, into life.

There is Ascent, up the mountain, to self-realization, and Descent, like Moses bringing the Ten Commandments—transmission—to people. We must bring this into life.

We must transmit to even one person, a bird even, a dog. What is not made alive is lost. Practice makes alive. Must practice—bring to the world.

Ascent and Descent are parts of the same energy, which is what flows through me. It is what we are. We are not educated rightly about this. We think that thoughts, feelings, reactions, like and dislike, are a problem. The aborigines in Australia do not think this way—all is one. (But they have other problems) [*smiles*].

So it is lawful to feel *dépassé* [*overwhelmed*], and that can orient me again to the life moving through me, which is all, contains all.

Seeing Allows
This Other Energy To Appear

What is the event of work? What we do is a preparation. To be very active, filled with conscious energy, in action, in movement. Seeing when mind takes over or feelings take over.

If it is "my" attention, it is not this other Attention, which transforms. Each moment can be an emergency to wish to be in relation again with this energy. Moral conscience to attend to that. Attraction to it. It is always there.

How to see, really see, myself as I am—hopeless, thinking, whatever.... *Seeing* allows this other energy to appear so I can be related to it. It changes everything. I don't care what's going on—thoughts, emotions. It can embrace everything.

Breathing—a mystery—finer breathing. Takes in *prana* [*life force*]. Not tricks, techniques, not to use breathing, but have respect for it, for the mystery, for the energy. The universe is breathing. Not my breathing. No body, no mind; just this stream.

Can I stay with the living mystery? Be responsible for being sensitive.

I am given life—am still given it. Only when I become conscious, aware of it, can it affect the quality of my manifestations. The living mystery…
I AM.

It Is the Inner Life That Breathes

When there is the intention to work, who "does" that? Who senses, sits in certain way? There are two "me's," one which is "me" and the world, "me" separate—and another "me" which begins to touch both worlds and is part of universal life.

There are stages:
First, *control*—
>wanting to control all the forces

Then, *uncertainty*—
>not sure what or how to be with these forces

Then, *submission*—
>just to submit to the attention and *be*

The attention is not yet pure to be completely aligned with this energy—no thoughts—needs the silence. Other vibrations are there perhaps, yet just to be attracted, so at moments [*eyes close, hand—in front of face—moving down*] to be one with this pure Attention.

And because of a feeling, breathing becomes different….

Breathe in… through the top of the head….
Breathe out… through the whole body….
Breathe in… through the axis of attention….
Breathe out… through the whole body….

Conscious breathing…. Different now because it is not the body that breathes. It is the inner life that breathes. And it is not this body but another body that receives.

Saturday

Every Hour, To Align

One confuses the senses with sensation. Sensation is another quality. Proprioceptive perception. Can have it voluntarily. This electrical circuit through us creates an event. When another energy contacts the body, a substance is liberated. There is a sensitive atmosphere. More subtle things can be perceived.

Without sensation, the impression is not received.

With sensation, the nature of the space changes. Feeling can penetrate, change the emanation.

Feeling—a very great thing. Must be prepared for it. A preparation of mind and body. Concentration permits this contact.

This morning, every hour, to align. Really feel this energy. Feel the whole.

And with it, the mysterious words, "Lord, have mercy."

Come Back to This Quiet in You

I look at myself and the world, and I see that it is ordinary. I renounce this look for another. Not to see but to join in this empty space….

Two feet… two knees… two elbows….
All parts balanced….
Three breaths….

And the activity quiets down in the brain. A new kind of breathing appears that helps steady me. A subtle axis, as if the axis of the world moves through me so that not a thought can stop it.

And the world is no longer an object—I am part of it. Not passive, the body, not alone by itself, but only as part of the whole human being does it have meaning. Only when animated by an attention.

So the body is tamed. The ox is herded. The body serves, is the servant of consciousness.

And I have a new perspective. Humility means dying to oneself. Not concerned with yesterday's state, comparing to today. Let the dead bury the dead. You are alive now. Your primary aim is to come back to this Attention, this quiet in you.

Awaken This Sense of Presence

There is a horizontal dimension and a vertical dimension. We must live in the horizontal, yes, because we are human beings on earth. But there can also be an attraction to this vertical dimension—can be like a magnet.

The vertical symbolism of the cross—you feel this when you are aligned. As soon as you separate, there is a witness. When aligned, there is no witness. The difficult thing is that the cross is also horizontal—to experience the movement of life. And this is the crucifixion—a very difficult thing.

Begin to be attracted there, to this vertical dimension [*moves hand down a few times in front of face*], related to it. Receiving an impression that creates this vertical relation.

Not for me, for my joy, for my pleasure, but—mysteriously—to awaken this sense of presence.

The Attention Is Always There

It's good to feel dissatisfaction that I don't correspond to the finer energy. That comes from an intelligence. At the moment I see my inadequacy, something can open.

Seeing: come into a relation with something that sees deeply inside.

But be pitiless with the one who is dissatisfied with the way things are. Be sensitive. Stay a while, so force enters: it must, if I try to *see*.

You don't have to be a certain way to be related to this energy. If you lay your framework on it—it's this, it's that—there will be remorse later. We are reminded, fortunately, because we are always mistaken.

Pure energy puts it all in order. Presence cures everything.

When related to this energy, I can abandon plans, images, forcing.

The Attention is always there—never disappears. The central attention, calling to me, just not listened to. The other attention hooks onto an object, thought, feeling, impression—but behind that can be the see-er, and behind that, the see-er—behind that, the see-er—until behind that—*nothing*.

Sunday

Freedom in a Moment

Freedom in a moment, freedom from fear and being anxious, freedom to be just as I am, giving all to what is number one in me.

To be able to close the shutters to everything else, and go deeply, instantaneously, into this central attention—and to respect that.

And in life, too, to do the things you want, to intensify the doing of them. Not to dream about them and have regret about them, but to try to do what you're inclined to do—and more intensely. Instead of doing it in thirty minutes, to do in five minutes.

This attention implanted in me is unknown. It can know its nature only when it is free, and this can happen only when it is free of "commitments." These commitments are various influences.

There are many forces that act through me but I don't see; I don't know where they lead. This other *seeing* is a force—a process—that acts through me.

It is only in this state of freedom which this seeing gives that I can care how I am. I must be free to care how I am.

The Only Way Out Is Up

Something is different. I know where I'm going.

I begin to be confident in this return to awareness of this energy—the source of peace and tranquility in me.

Movements show body as second but vital, the instrument that serves. Unexpectedly, feelings are touched by consciousness.

Intelligence of the heart appears.

Real attention. Real *I*. Simple. Humble. Open to the world. Let it be.

> *The whole of me breathing….*
> *Through the upper part of the head….*
> *Through the spine….*
> *Through the solar plexus….*
> *Seven breaths, each lighter…..*

Listen… to life in this moment.

When I'm not listening, attending to the life in this body now, in every cell, it's like a string is cut. I fall down. And the only way out is up.

Love Is Not a Speech about Love

There is a secretary of the mind, filled with ideas, but it has no relation to the subconscious, can't understand it.

Love is not a speech about love—quite another experience.

How to develop sustained attention? Have passion. To respect this energy, to be passionate about it. To be related to this energy, to let the forces move through you. To serve this energy and bring it to earth.

Allow myself the rigor to align more and more with this greater force. Love is one aspect of it.

Not to be a professor, an expert in the culture of carrots, alone in her room, but manifesting in the world. What good is a teacher without students? There is the need for something to pass, to circulate. The light, moving always through everything. No ideas about it.

Pulled here and there, yes—but to come back because you are passionate about it. Like being in love: you don't want to be separated from this. All in service to this energy. Let it come in. Love it. "Passionating" in it.

Everything Feeds
This Sense of Presence

This is a new stage of work, receiving all impressions coming in. And the world has new interest. It is like riding a horse through a new country—everything is brand new, everything is of interest. Everything feeds this sense of presence.

Living in it more and more…. It begins to work in you. But the closer to the king, the greater the sin if you betray it, if you just let it go. You have been given the sacred—remarkable experiences—so it is your responsibility to make it possible for that experience to happen again and again.

You know how. Let it penetrate you fully. It is the most important thing. Perhaps you must give up this or that in a moment, so you can receive. It's all ephemeral anyway—it's *not you.* You are getting in the way of it when a thought or reaction of the moment takes the attention.

You can serve this energy. Even when things flame up in you. You have an aim. You can be the servant. Like the shoe salesman in the store who knows he is there only to sell shoes. A man comes in with his friend—full of ego, talking, says things—but it does not matter to the shoe salesman. He is there only to sell shoes [*smiles*]. Oh, maybe later he makes a comment….

If you're not serving, you're not working. If you are serving, you are working.

WEEK THREE

Monday

To Serve This Intelligence

I need to have the intention to be an instrument of higher Intelligence, to serve that. Why is work necessary?

Man is incomplete, unfinished (why you feel a lack). Man has a responsibility—necessary to take responsibility—for his place in the bigger picture. When a man works, he can see and feel the effect on others.

The work needs you. Not sentimental. *The work needs you.* Now. In this moment. And when you are needed, you can find extraordinary energy. If just for you, can put off until tomorrow, but if you feel needed, you are called. You appear. If there is a fire in the house or the subway doors are closing, instantly you go, you appear, you know what to do; you go to it immediately.

The jungle grows up quickly every day. Must make a path every day. For many years we try methods, but then a sensitivity appears, an intelligence. I see that I must adjust to that, to correspond to that.

The rest—tricks, work habits—artificial things—at first can bring you to the door, but now, let them go. Not to be aware of just this or that but to be aware of everything.

The work: to be related to this energy. First, self-consciousness. Then, objective consciousness. To be related to Self—to *I*. To open directly. To work instantaneously—now. To have the intention to serve this Intelligence. To be a channel for that, more and more in life.

Be "In the Middle"

These ups and downs we go through when we are self-centered—necessary suffering. But it is quite extraordinary to have moments of feeling a part of this work.

We are all like this, experiencing associations, frustrations—with good reason: look at what you've done today. To let that be, but to feel some pure attention, free of associations, even as you are, suffering, tired—a beautiful landscape! So remarkable when there is, along with that, a moment of attention—quite different. And the seeing, this contact with pure attention, is freeing.

When I am aware of this axis in me, am there "in the middle," none of the forces of life—reaction, thought, feeling—can take me away. When I vibrate with this higher energy, this axis in me, I am invulnerable to the forces of this world.

It is better—more alive—to be "in the middle" than even gladness in achieving presence. See when and what forces take me away from attending to presence, see all the aspects of the "difficulty": the sense of "I AM" and then what happens to take me away—and the return.

Something goes and returns. That's the way it is. Two worlds. Only in the center do the two worlds meet. When in this axis, I can naturally open to the world.

Meditation is only a preparation. The highest is action. Bringing this quality into life—very difficult—so both levels coexist, this alignment with something greater, something absolutely greater than myself that shows what the body is for, and at the same time, bringing this into life.

To be related inside, of course, but also to let this relation come into manifestations. This is what is needed. This is the action that is needed.

Join This World of Presence

Seeing *what is*—what permits to *see*?

There is an ascending movement toward a sensitivity, a receptivity. I begin to see, to receive an energy, to have respect for it. I can be a slave or I can support it. It is interesting to see how I go away from that and return to that. I can even ask, how is it I become indifferent to that?

Not to withdraw to be in the higher regions, isolated. Not to be taken by life.

Accept the oscillations of consciousness and continue to attend to presence.

Our experience of consciousness is not for our own satisfaction but to bring consciousness into life, animate these forms. From this, our true individuality comes.

If I try for presence from some egoistic aim rather than to genuinely serve it, respect its power, attend to it—it vanishes, and instead, there is manipulation, compromise, pretense. But when I genuinely wish to join this world of presence just to be in contact with it, it will always come.

The Now Contains Everything

The Now—not a time but a place, the central core, the *axis mundi* [*axis of the world*] in me.

There is the higher and my functioning. Feeling I can't or I am not related to that higher—something is demanded of me. Let the two forces meet. They are universal forces, and they will meet, and one will become active, one passive. You don't need to "do" anything but let them meet. Only, abandon this thought that "I can't," and just let be.

Acceptance—just as it is. Permitting a space. Recognizing this unknown force appearing, this higher Intelligence. Not knowing what it is, but letting it work through me. And something new and miraculous appears.

"Now"—beyond time. The Now contains the answers to all questions.

The Now contains everything.

Tuesday

Resistance Is
Just Being Engaged Elsewhere

Resistance is really not that. It is an unconscious competition. There is natural resistance but all that means is just being engaged elsewhere, committed elsewhere. Like the child on the playground when the teacher calls. Not that the child has resistance but he is engaged elsewhere.

It is natural to protect oneself from threats from the outside. But there is nothing inside that "resists." All there is, is the absence of free attention so attention is attached to this and that.

Why is there "resistance"? Because work is truth, and takes away one's illusions, one's security.

Resistance in you—must go through this, of course, it's normal. But it's from thinking, "I'm something." If it's up to me, of course I cannot do it—I cannot be God—so resistance. But everything is done *through* me, if I allow it.

We need an empty space, and then this force, this higher force that comes in, is irresistible. Once I think I can "do" it, it's finished. But to be in the place between the two—myself and this force, this unknown appearing. Not to pretend and not to withdraw like a coward.

When the sun is there, I am positive. There is no resistance. When the sun is hidden behind clouds, I have faith that it is there.

Am I That?

Recognizing you are far away, ask, *Am I that?* The question helps you join again with what you are—this energy—so it seems even childish to be identified with this small thing. *Am I that?*

Even seeing it in a poor state, not animated, a lump, all this unnecessary stuff, but just to see. Let it be. Self-containment: keep inside yourself. See these other things come back—no need to manifest—but ask, *Am I that?*

We have different states:

passive—nothing there
observing—better; a kind of psychological
    state, seeing this or that behavior
higher seeing—best; doesn't matter what is seen;
    you are more awake, in this finer energy

What is "the self"? The self is my attention. Just that. Where is my attention? Where my attention is, that is where I am, that is my self.

When the attention is with this other energy, everything opens to this. Like seeing a child's smile, or someone suffering—the heart opens.

When the energy is here, there is clarity—like a clear window. Perhaps there is a demand from outside. Like a fire on a hillside. I just go where I am needed, because of this clarity. Otherwise, there is scheming and manipulating. But one can be clear. One can *be.*

There Are Two Kinds of Self-Love

Animate all of you: mind, feelings, body. Be with this energy as you move in life. Relations with people—different—companions in search.

A demand here brings my three parts together, not yet harmonized, but together.

There is a higher part in myself that I can be with—a new balance—rather than being with the usual. Can let that be but remain with this higher part that receives energy from Above, like a wave of goodness, love. When concentrated, attentive to this higher part, can see—deeper seeing. Otherwise, I go down into the ordinary—objects—partial—cannot see.

There are two kinds of self-love: ordinary self-love, selfish, reactive, all the projections of the mind; and love of Self, from the higher part, from Above, like the sun that warms every part—not judge—benevolent. There is reverence toward this unconditional love.

You feel this shower of energy in you—makes you tender—this process working in you. Parts come together, can receive something, a most refined energy. Can be calm. Impressions come *to* you rather than you go out to impressions, objects. Instead, you emanate.

Must be very active, open and watchful. Let the process work in you, these emanations work in you.

Whether there is joy, or impressions of another, or the body doing this or that, all is seen, permeated, when the attention can remain, when this subtle energy can be felt to be present, too—the main focus.

Wednesday

When There Is a Relation with the Source

Attention is an intelligence that comes into me, the representative in me of the sacred, the higher. The ascending movement toward myself. What active correspondence is required of me?

Realize that you cannot "do" it. You cannot do anything. You cannot transform yourself no matter how much you try. There is the old man and the new man. Two completely different creatures.

But when there is a relation with the Source, the new man appears, and everything is different, and you know it. There is no more "me, me." You can see it in the face. This is not the case when the relation is not there.

Begin to awaken, and this Intelligence appears, deep intelligence. Not from the mind, not psychological. Then, to recognize it, to respect it, to keep it intact. Responsible for that. See the subjective thoughts, functions, yes—but to return to this empty space between two thoughts, between two acts.

Life Helps You Work

Life helps you work. The richness of life helps you work. Not to be dominated by reaction, ego, wish to control.

Not asking what's missing, wanting it to be like this or that, so you make it like this or that—it's finished. But just [*finger in front of forehead, eyes close, finger moves straight down*] to be in the silence, centered in it.

Sometimes you are not completely taken. Like the moment in bed before sleep, reviewing your day without reaction. An important moment, at night, before you fall asleep. Look at how your day was—when you were aggressive with people. Looking at it all impartially gives you the taste of someone who can see all this without reacting.

The central attention is the main thing.

Everything else is second. Not the body. Not the "glove." This central attention: a force in me. Not reactive.

"To accept" means this central attention is there.

That which accepts grows stronger. For moments, I am nearer the see-er, That which sees. A subtle vibration appears, and I can trust that.

With this comes the richness of life.

Pay with Your Attention

What is payment? What is sacrifice?

Payment is simple, concrete: to give what is necessary. To give what is necessary to climb the path, to make a person flower, to get into the cinema. When things go wrong, what didn't I do—pay—that could have made it better? Pay with your attention.

Sacrifice has a practical meaning, too. Sacrifice means to make sacred. Not "morality" but like the Hindu ritual of throwing *soma* [*psychoactive elixir*] into the fire. All my vital forces, features, get thrown into the fire of consciousness—and blazing up from all this comes real *I*. Like *soma* in the fire—lights me up with life.

I sacrifice my self-pity. I respond to a call. Self-pity—pernicious—colors so much, but when there is this inner core, attending it, you are not taken. I sacrifice something in this moment so something higher lives.

Work is sacrifice. You must die to feel the presence of the mountains. In this looking, there is a dying to all these aspects that keep us slaves.

And clarity comes. The central attention is there, does not wish to go into automatic behavior.

There begins to be a preference for consciousness.

Speak from the Love of It

When speaking in a meeting, give just the essence of your experience, the principle about work you have discovered, not the details.

Much stronger to present just the essence.

Must be sensitive to the atmosphere of the group and help us to be together in work.

This word, that word, does not matter as much as feeling, in each moment, the call to something. Called to something higher.

To really see and know oneself well, to feel the necessity of this relationship with the finer, the living mystery—to open to the universe, see myself more deeply—then what words come can transmit and penetrate.

You must feel the necessity in yourself of being related to this energy—the *need* to see. Then what you say to others can transmit something.

This energy is discovering me. Be prudent about describing it to yourself as one thing or another—or wanting it again. If I have an experience the same for a hundred times, then maybe I can say that is nature.

How to preserve the wolf and sheep, both intact? Does the functioning devour the contact with finer energy?

When speaking, don't consider. Just begin. In the silence. Speak from the love of it, and the words will come. If talking becomes ordinary, it will have no action. But if you respect and love this energy, you are called again.

Align with this energy. Simple. Natural. This relationship is everything—most important—and then to bring it into life.

Thursday

Come Under Another Influence

We are on a journey together, all of us. Some are in advance, some behind, but all the same. We are in a process. A process to come under another influence. Of the Self.

Once we come under this influence, body and mind gladly obey. On this trip, we become human beings. Human beings have this transcendent dimension.

The sin of Lucifer: the pride of existing separately from the whole, from God. A shame of another kind arises, from the Higher—not from me, not personal—that asks, *What is needed to repair that?*

It is good to try to see things from a higher perspective—not me, mine, but a more objective perspective when asking what it's all about. See myself as a human being among human beings.

Some moments we are taken by things. Rise above. See humanity, what it's doing and what for. How can we understand what is a conscious beehive—humanity—which produces a substance? This substance is the only one that can attract the *I*. We are all the same. There is no difference. We must come together to produce this substance.

This Mutually Freer State

We have a need. Maybe it is not felt. We must practice. And when there is a real need, and I cannot meet it, there is suffering. I know then it is a real need. Suffering permits something to be received, to go beyond one's limits.

Work leaders are not gods. If a teacher is not indicating something beyond him, he is not a teacher. Sometimes—weakness—trust broken. If we are suffering, in grief, to let that be. We are responsible to each other to get through this.

People have different challenges they must go through to mature. Suffering: allow it to take place, but remember what you have, what is behind. Challenge is necessary. Something purer can come, a clearing out, receiving new force—compassion—

When a misunderstanding occurs, from that can come the opportunity to correct oneself more deeply, see that one needs to be more sensitive, pure.

With true transmission, the exchange flows in both directions.

Needs very active attention, a new quality of attention and receptivity, permitting the flow of knowledge both ways. If one way only, dependence appears—on memories, associations—rather than this mutually freer state.

See that all life is in me when I am in this central attention. And for teachers, all pupils are the same: orient them upward. A sign that I am in this central attention: see all people the same, like me, have this energy, this Intelligence.

The work cannot be given by words, ideas—not "transmitted" in groups—but in receiving, in the silence, this Impression.

The Interloper and the
One Who Is Aligned

Maybe you are still too personal, too self-centered. But the lower world is not you, though you belong to it. We must recognize again that we are two. The interloper and the one who is aligned.

See how at one moment there can be excessive praising of yourself, and at another, wanting to be reassured how great you are. Who is looking at it? If there's a show, [*smiles*] we don't have to go to the movies!

Giving coffee to someone—just a movement of this world, it's not you—impersonal when something is awakened. But you appropriate it and speculate about it and make something out of it. Always trapped by that.

So there are all these levels of seeing myself. At certain moments if someone looks at me, sometimes the interloper reacts in me, but something goes through to the other one who is just receiving impressions directly. Something else is touched.

Little by little, a sense of another kind of *seeing* appears, which brings unity.

Seeing God's creation. Contemplation of creation. To really serve. To create such an animation in the world. This would have an action.

Friday

Let a Feeling Arise for Consciousness

Being with the greatness of nature, another quality appears, another self, connected to something outside time and space. The joy you feel—not for you but to connect you, as in prayer.

The feelings that come with attention allow this finer energy to work in you.

The Attention is what is behind everything. The feeling of joy when awake in this energy is natural, because suddenly you are part; you have your place in it.

The body is quiet now, and it likes this quietness.

There may be some busyness in the mind; let it be. I know better now where to retire from that more and more. Let a feeling arise for consciousness. Let this feeling arise....

Breathe in... through the top of the head....
Breathe out... through the whole body....

Now… lighter… we come to a place of non-effort. Natural. No words. A place of real peace.

Agitation around me does not affect that.

There is an axis in myself of this energy, this presence… in the silence…. And I am aware of the direction of the inexhaustible dimension of Attention.

Recognize This Energy

This sensitivity to a flowing in of fine energy…. Like pregnancy: you carry something, a life inside you that's precious. You wish to preserve it, protect it, not to do this or that silly thing. Recognize directly this energy in me; be sensitive to it.

Sensitivity allows *I* to appear in the body. I have images of myself, how I should be. Just let it be as it is and observe. Each moment opens into the unknown. The sense of separation between myself and the world dissolves. The lightness changes my being. It gives me another sense of myself. In a way, I don't recognize myself.

In seeing comes the purification—everything can be there in this. All useful—ego, automatism, personality—to walk, to talk—but also to recognize this energy again, align again. No struggle. Maybe in the beginning struggle produces an energy that allows seeing to begin, but once there is seeing, once there is the recognition of this energy, no struggle.

Not to change anything, but to see. Trying to "do" something is a compulsion, a distraction. We always think we have to "do." *Just recognize.*

A Demand on Oneself To Appear

What is real *I*? When is it unmistakably present so I know I am here, and all the parts submit?

When it appears, it is irresistible. Like someone coming in through the door—all the attention is drawn to that person. All the forces go toward that. It is not one of the little I's that tries.

[*Michel's dog paws at the door to be let out.*]
Like our state. Always wanting to go out.
If I go too far away, hard to bring back.

[*Michel calls to the dog, who responds.*]
I am sensitive only when I am called.
Then I appear.

I am thankful for a demand from outside because it shows me I have something to give. Like a mother who nurses: the milk comes only when there is a demand.

To make a demand on oneself is an intelligent thing to do; a demand to appear.

I need an aim. I need to make a decision, in this circumstance or that, in front of this person in the dining room, or wherever, to see how I am.

Without this, I am just passive. But I don't want to be stupid. I don't want to spend the energy in just any old way.

It is necessary to work with intensity for a short period each day, go deeply inside. Into the quiet. Become collected, related. Then for the rest of the time, to go about one's business, perhaps carry something.

Is It Possible Now?

A demand on myself brings more sensitivity so a quality appears, and I am completely different. The movement of life becomes more vivid.

Letting it be permits transformation. We can never change things about ourselves, none of us can. Yet in moments there can be transformation.

To let the seeing appear, deeply appear, when reactive, when groping, while letting it be just as it is, and asking, *Now, what is needed?*

A question is the subtlest form of demand. To see my human condition. To be in both forces: this energy that is there, and this body. All questions come from this division, these differences of levels, ordinary life and the higher. All questions, really, are about how to get from here to there.

A real question calls the attention. Like a life-and-death matter: "Should I marry her?" It calls the attention immediately. It is like that.

Your question to be a real question must quiet the mind. It must be a question the mind cannot answer. So the mind questions, then steps back.

Instead of believing in thoughts, to step out of the way, so this Intelligence works through you.

Asking a real question (not from thought) has in it a taste of this state one asks about. Not, "How to do that?" (that's cheap), but ask, *Is it possible now*?

Saturday

Let This Flow of Life Penetrate

This work is not for you. You are for this work. Man cannot "do," but without you, it cannot be done.

Danger calls me. I see that my work is in danger, and so I come back, join again this axis of attention.

Can I liberate myself from all the illusory thoughts? For this I need free attention. To feel the call. To join with that which is always within me. To join with that because it is more real. It is always there—doesn't need energy, doesn't take energy. But when I am joined with it, great energy enlivens me.

I don't know who I am but I am full of dreams— dreams of work, even. Why am I alive? I am unachieved. What does it mean, a new birth? Most important: who is it that witnesses?

Today we are more capable, more related, so not to get caught in details—"why did he do that," "she said that"—not to be lost in any little thing, but to hear the call. Come to what is essential, this unknown, this mystery. To stay in concentration, not go far away from myself but to let this flow of life penetrate me more deeply.

Today, to protect something essential. And to share life. Perhaps I can begin to come closer to the question: *Who am I?*

In the Silence, Wish Can Appear

To have a general overview, one must climb higher. There are aids—ropes of silence.

In the silence there can be a fire that animates a part that is never animated.

In the silence, wish can appear. I can't wish, but in the silence, wish can arise.

To be related inside like this—with an axis of inner silence as a core…. Impressions come in but do not dominate. Greed, avarice, self-pride, cunning, all can be there but they are innocuous, do not dominate, even can serve.

Impressions come in; the impulse to go out to some object, some situation; but the attention is primary. I join with this Attention, like a thread of energy from Above.

Sensitive to the Attention Behind

I take myself exactly as I am. Change nothing. See *what is.*

Acceptance is what is needed. With acceptance, there is energy for something more. Something is given. Something opens. Direct reception from higher Intelligence.

I see that I am coarse, brutal, with no sensitivity, no opening. So I open to this energy. It makes me sensitive. It educates me. It informs me. It brings feeling. Let it be in every cell.

The Attention "behind"—be sensitive to it. A certain "density" of Attention and then you want to be in relation to That. You are tolerant because not pulled so. You can let it be inside and outside.

Emotions pull me this way and that, feed the mind. I need to see that.

But when present, when awake: peace with oneself. I can have tolerance, compassion for others because I'm not perfect. I'm here, attracted to this certain Attention behind. This feeling can provide the energy needed for objective thought, as if objective thought were just waiting for that energy needed for it to appear.

A very active attention keeps me related to this "density" of Attention, of presence. I need to be sensitive to the Attention behind.

The Real Force in Me

Where is the real force in me? I must recognize it, so I am not always looking to the outside. This force—attention, presence—to have a sensation of it. Attentive every instant.

What should we serve? This higher Intelligence in us. When I have a feeling of being far away from this, it is good because it calls me near, to go toward that again. It is a help, this feeling of being far away from it. It can bring sensitivity, can open me to receive this finer energy. Not taken by the impulses of the head.

Now that you have been worked on by conditions, the attention is voluntary. Today, not to depend on anything from the outside, but to see the non-correspondence to this energy, and each one, to find his way to correspond to it.

The attention can be free of the body. When I recognize this Attention more and more, there can be a certain calm around it. Nothing can disturb it. This axis in me is essential. The body becomes a kind of channel for the force so that it can pass—free—independent.

And so there appears a tender feeling for the world.

Sunday

Nothing Belongs to Me

Nothing which I call "me"—thoughts, feelings, reactions—is mine. *Not one thing.* The same is true for everyone. Fears, desires, wishes, yes, all this goes on but…. Is this body yours? You are given this body, but is it yours?

Nothing belongs to me—not even when I go to the bathroom, *that* is not mine. Yes, I can witness my functions, but nothing belongs to me. Not eating. Not even the ideas about work. The ideas are "mine" only when they are experienced, and then that permits an understanding of them.

In life, there are many kinds of bait. The ideas are a kind of bait, from a loving source, for a purpose.

Don't identify with the bait.

Let everything go.

Recognize this Intelligence appearing. It knows better than you. Receive it. Join it. Respect it.

Everything else, the "I" that thinks, believes, feels this or that—all identification. That one is stupid—flattered—pretentious—controlling. Yet I respect that one, too, this companion that is always with me but is not me. I can even have conversations with it—but it is not me.

Have an axis of attention, collected, central in me, intact. From that, all will take its proper place.

Nothing belongs to me except that which recognizes my true nature. When I can see this—this is freedom of the *I*. It is a great liberation. And I come to live under a new influence.

When nobody pretends to own this Attention, it can know its Source.

When Something Real Is Received,
Wish Arises

There is something about the silence of a hundred people who have a certain education, more than the silence of two or three people. There is also something about the agitation of a hundred people [*smiles*]. Can see the agitation around adults.

But it is so striking when people are very quiet, turned toward what calls them "innerly" and *not at all taken* by whatever is around them. Each face becomes beautiful. And it is lost as soon as that quietness is not in them.

And it is good to receive this impression, for we wish to have an aim, a double aim, to be related both to what is inside—which gives meaning, openness—and to the world. To be in relationship with both.

When something real is received, by grace, then a wish arises. Like falling in love: there must be a relation; then it is felt, real. Any other "wish" is illusion, abuse of the word.

There is no *wish* without relation. A wish is based on something real. The wish to serve That.

Opening to the Unknown Frees Me

Sadness, perhaps, which arises. Pity. Compassion maybe. This sensitivity has brought greater awareness of *what is.* See this suffering—me—others. Deep wounds from the moment we come into the world. Yet healing takes place from this energy when I'm in relation with it.

Mystics speak of being one with God. There are degrees, approaches to the Absolute, intermediaries (Jesus, Buddha). When I begin to be open, to leave an open space, I begin to have a relation with an energy, a vibration, come closer.

Opening to the unknown frees me from all the known mechanisms. Not to be identified, pulled from this central attention by identification with anything that arises.

And in this relation, I am transformed so an even finer vibration can fill—can be in relation with—and then, an even finer one.

Be Fully a Channel for That

The true self is God in you. Receiving actively is all.

You are in between—that is good. You do not need to understand or to try. It is mysterious, not knowing. The more I try, the more the door is shut.

> *We are at the door.*
> *"Who is it?"*
> *"Me."*
> *The door remains closed.*
> *"Who is it?"*
> *"ME!"*
> *The door remains closed.*
> *"Who is it?"*
> *"I am Thou."*
> *And the door opens….*

Let us be really aligned so much that we don't exist separately. You are not alone. There is a network always, actively working, since the dawn of humanity. Offering reminders. And you can come near to it.

Now you belong to something. You are part of something. All the human strivings: realize what they are. Create a link with this network of influence.

You are Buddha.
You are God.

Needing all your care to be fully a channel for that. And you know the way to this. This energy creates love in you, creates consciousness in you. But it needs your care, your *full care*.

YOU CAN RECEIVE THE WHOLE WORLD:
A Talk with Young People

Once you have a taste of the relation with this energy, you begin to see what is unnecessary and let it go. Not to let the mind go here and there, now, out of respect for this energy, for attending to it. It is your fundamental activity.

If the mind starts to think about this or that—not necessary now—let it go. Out of respect for this energy, you come back. You are attracted there.

In this work, first it is necessary to become balanced in all parts. Sensing the body... and the feelings join... and the mind. Balanced for a moment, the force equally in all parts. This is normal man.

And then, one can become conscious of one's functions. It is a training. Our functions are our companions. They need to be educated. The mind is like a dog—always chewing on a bone—very short thoughts, one after the other. But it can be trained, so that you can come back to this axis in you, this centeredness, so you can *be*.

And the feelings, too. So there is a reaction. I allow it to be but at the same time come back to this centeredness. What is this reaction? Is it important? And perhaps I see that it is nothing—fear of this or wishing for that.

But the primary thing is this relation with an energy, to become a channel for it.

There are two men in you. There is the one who when he is centered, when he is in relation to something, is totally different, can do anything, is intense, alive, generous. And then, at another moment, back in my usual state, with my resistance, thoughts, reactions. The one who thinks he is in charge, controlling everything—fears this, wishes that, all my problems. Can let him go for a moment. Relax him, too. Leave him at the door.

We cannot change ourselves. But when we are related to this energy inside us, it is a miracle. The goodness of it pours through me and changes everything.

You have a wish in you, but you are not aware of it. You have an energy in you, and when you are in relation with it, this axis of attention can stay longer, stay by itself even, because it is fed by every impression.

When this centeredness is there, you can receive the whole world. There is a calm, a quietness. A Look upon me, not from my ordinary self, but from That which sees objectively as it is. We are never fooled; something always knows what we do.

When listening to others speak, maybe this one sounds pretentious, can unbalance you, but you listen as if you are in front of the unknown.

The more free the attention, the more you receive.

You can find that place in you that can let it be.

Let it be. This axis of energy accepts—acceptance is "energetical"—and does not wish anything to be different, accepts to be where I am.

Who am I? We work to know who we are.

Without this axis, this centeredness, this relation—our birthright—there is incompleteness.

This incompleteness calls me.

AFTERWORD:
A Great Gift

It is a great gift, to receive impressions. To taste impressions. To join with something very natural in our deepest nature.

We can then forgive all misunderstanding between human beings.

When the attention is with this other energy permeating me—very concentrated yet very light, free, wishing nothing, needing nothing—everything is put into order naturally. Everything takes its proper place. Everything opens to this—the head, the heart.

And this energy is still not the highest. It is "The Boss" but not yet "The Superboss." This first stage is important because this force, this energy I perceive when awake, is the child of another higher energy that, perhaps, will come.

There is a great cycle. A higher Intelligence coming down to meet the impressions of life. To be here on earth is to be part of this universal life, to be a channel for this energy. It is a new love affair, a new marriage of forces, receiving this energy so it can penetrate deeper and work through you. It is not of the body or the functions, has nothing to do with that. And it can open you.

We can become sensitive to a quality that dwells within us, among us. This attention in me can know its Source.

Can I liberate myself from all my concerns and enter the mystery? For this I need free attention. Free from all my concerns. The mystery is always there, from the first moment to the last.

At moments, abandon everything.

Enter it.